Confessions

An excerpt for me, an excerpt for you, an excerpt for everything we've been through

Priyam Agarwal

India | USA | UK

Made with ❤ on the BookLeaf Publishing Platform
www.bookleafpub.in
www.bookleafpub.com

Dedication

To Myself
My love, light and life comes from me

Preface

Before I began writing this book, I had a lot of strong feelings that I just wanted to pour on paper. As I put my pen on the paper, I realized all it needed was words and an honest heart to get through it.

Now, after completing it, I can confidently say that this book will find its way to the right hands. As you read this piece, I hope you find the words for all the noise that is inside you and it reaches your heart, just like it did mine.

Acknowledgements

Confessions

I'm a preaching Saint
With skeletons in my closet
I pretend to be what I ain't
A sinner posing as a Prophet

My confessions are painted Crimson
As I try to wash away my past
I'm Mary who isn't a Virgin
With clouds of my indiscretions cast

And I, like Anthony of the play
Orate my falls from graces
I beg to not live another day
As the fiends utter praises

Where Jesus turned water to wine
And the Greeks drank wine like water
I sat in between and prepared to dine
To feed on the innocents' laughter

Little did they know they'll be Gods someday
Looked up to repent the mortals' lapses
But they're flawed, not diamond but just clay
That makes once and twice collapses

Stars

I wait for a star to fall
For I've fallen from my graces
I wish for a wish as I'm appalled
I wish to be rid of my traces

I wait for a star to fall
For I've fallen into an abyss
I call for my Calling's call
A call for forlorn bliss

I wait for a star to fall
For I've fallen into a trap
Where I lay morbid and mauled
By the virtue of my mishap

I wait for a star to fall
I close my eyes and pray
To the one I don't believe in at all
To cast my soul away

Last Letter

Is this going to be my last letter?
Is this all I've left to say?
My fingers walk the edge, to test
The dagger in this play.

I spill the words on these blurry lines
Or will I spill my blood today?
So beautiful, so raw
Like wine on the parchment, they say.

The sheet absorbs, my sins absolve
Like a wilted flower I lay
Will you burn me in lands unknown?
Or will I rot another day?

Food for thought, I'll be food for worms
If you bury me instead
A wasted life I may have had
Could I be useful when I'm dead?

Scars

I often imagine my scars
As beautiful as the stars
And as I join them, in motion,
It completes me, a constellation

You can take a piece of me, as a token
And make a wish, for I'm broken
And say that I'm beautiful, from a distance
Until you reach me, and I burn you that instant

And tell little ones, that's what they become when
people leave
A graveyard for souls, the galaxies
A morbid fairy land or something of that sort
The stardust is nothing but a rotting corpse

They'll think their whole lives of becoming one
themselves
Only to realize that they need be dead
And then they'll learn there's beauty in death
The night sky is nothing but the goner's bed

Seed

The sun still shines, the rain still falls
It's got the light and love, that it needs
Yet the flower won't grow, and I don't know
The land isn't barren, damaged isn't the seed

Don't you want to see the world?
I wait for you to grow, I beg, I plead
It chooses to stay, like 'tis not mud but clay
My head just hurts, my heart just bleeds

The seed is I , or I'm the seed
Won't flower, won't frolick, won't feed
For we know the day we bloom oh so fine
Be plucked, decorated for someone's greed

But oh, dear oh, I still want to see the world
Come out, come out, it's all for you to see
Yet it chose to stay, like 'tis not mud but clay
My head just hurts, my heart just bleeds

Mirror

I look in the mirror a 100 times
Are the girl and I, the same?
We are separated by a mercurial line
I guess I've forgotten her name.

I look in the mirror a 100 times
To find her nth flaw
My defects are hers, her blemishes are mine
I see her wounds, still raw.

I look in the mirror a 100 times
Wishing I could look at her more
But I'm loomed over with an ominous sign
She's not the one I'm meant to adore.

I look in the mirror for one last time
The girl isn't the same, I believe
I break the glass as the clock struck 9
When I hurt myself, she bleeds.

Wishes

I wish I could be, the dreams that you see
Gently guiding your heart, tender and free
I wish I could be, the stars up above
Showering you softly with endless love

Oh how I wish I could be, the warmth of your smile
Embracing your spirit, if only for a while
Yet in this quiet yearning, I ponder and find
Do you share the desires that flicker in my mind?

My Life is a Book

My life's a book
A neverending story
Full of drama
And gore and glory

I invite you to read me
Or be a chapter
I promise you'll lay
Amazed and enraptured

Because not only I
Have a fable to tell
It's surreal and unreal
And would put you under spell

So be my guest
Please grab a corner
Flip through the pages
And stand enamoured

Enemy

I am my own enemy
Watering fresh dreams
With stale efforts

I am my own foe
Reaping the fruits of
The dead seeds I sow

I am my own rival
Dying of thirst
But trying to drown first

I am my own nemesis
A perpetual decadent
A fool, A pessimist

Pretty Things

Oh pretty things
Take me instead and
Make me you

Oh pretty things
I hate the colors and
I'm feeling blue

Oh pretty things
How does it feel to get
The attention of the lovers?

Oh pretty things
Will I ever get noticed
Beyond the shell that covers?

My Story

I'll lay my story in blood one day
My pain dripping through the words
You tell my life's a boon, my friend
I guess I was the curse

I'll lay my story in blood one day
And then you'll know why
I have few friends and I tend to end
Every happiness that comes by

Mourn

We are gathered here to mourn
The death of my dreams
An end of the era of
Could-be's and Have-been's

We are gathered here to mourn
The demise of my hopes
Feel free to shed a few tears
Feel free to mope

We are gathered here to mourn
The passing of my sanity
As I get comfortable around
Pain and profanity

So gather around and tell
My friends I meant well
I will be back someday my love
But until then, farewell.

Brown

Brown was the tree trunk
That we hugged when we played
Brown were the leaves in autumn
Delicate and frayed

Brown was the moth
That couldn't stay away from the fire
Brown was the bed
Of my grandfather's pyre

Brown were things
that the poets made poetic
Brown is the colour of my skin
Then why is it not accepted?

No Blue Skies

If tomorrow our sky is no longer blue
What if the world ends, we'd have no clue
Just a day, to pay our dues
A day to paint the picture, that our lives drew

If tomorrow our sky is no longer blue
I wish I knew what I'd do
Will I hold you tight or bid you adieu
Make up for the lost time, long overdue

If tomorrow our sky is no longer blue
Whispers of laughter that once felt so true
In the silence, I'll search for a sign anew
Hoping tomorrow, I find my way to you

Photos

I have no photos in my phone
Of things I've loved or people I've known
Not that I mean that I'm alone
I guess I've grown
Out of the memories thrown
My way, now I atone
The mistakes, I disown

If you feel sad for me, don't
There's nothing to remember
Nothing to bemoan
So I stare at the screen
Trying to find skeletons, or just bones
Trying to find a photo, in my phone.

Man in the Building

He's just a man in the building
What would you make of it
He's got a beautiful wife
And a now 20-year old kid.

He's just a man in the building
Who seems up and about
No one wonders what he does
Maybe there's no reason for a doubt.

He's just a man in the building
Hungry eyed, hovering hands
"Come play little girl, I won't hurt you"
Says he, watching where he stands.

He's just a man in the building
As he grabs the little prey
Fondling the 9-year old
Trying to have his way.

He's just a man in the building
That's how she knows him today
His head held down as he passes her by
For he knows she knew what happened that day.

Heathen

I am a heathen, I have no God
A few call me eccentric, a few call me odd.
I'm a lowly being, a pagan, barbarian
I believe in the beliefs of the contrarians.

So when I die, adorn my coffin with heathers
The casket made of aged wood and scattered with a few
feathers
Lay my box down in the land where I danced
Cross with the crucifix of my sacred trance.

My death will not be a passing, it will be a massacre
For I am a wild flower, trampled and tattered
And the curtains will fall when I close my eyes
They say a star falls when someone dies.

Entity

I'm a kindred spirit
Delicately fierce to keep
I love too much or not at all
But I wouldn't dive in too deep.

I'm a familial soul
Born at a dawn that flickered death
Running through life, or away from it
Not a moment to catch some breath

I'm a relative ghost
Standing at the doomed doors of life
A rope, a chair and not one care
A dagger, a blade, a knife.

Wreath

I weave a wreath today
I wonder where it will lay
On the mantle for festivities
Or on someone's grave

I weave a wreath today
Of wildflowers, purple and blue
The colours, my favourite
I hope you like them too

I weave a wreath today
And as I sleep it's upon me
I have been gone yet another day
The flowers dried ago eternity

I weave a wreath today
With the ones who once lived
We're forgotten, we're frayed
From the fickleness of memories made

Broken Things

They say broken things have beauty too
I abide by it, so dutiful
For I am cracked, and scarred, and shattered
I guess all of that, never mattered

Like when the light breaks
It's seven colors
And when we do
We break for others

A tear here, a tear there
The tears tearing me up anywhere
So I wipe them, and dust the knee
I welcome you to be my company

We break together, and we fall
You be my band-aid, I be your gauge
We'll fix each other, it'll be okay
And leave the misery, for another day

They say broken things have beauty too
I abide by it, so dutiful
For I am cracked, and scarred, and shattered
I guess all of that, never mattered

You are Art

You are the heart's whisper
In the stillness of the night
The secret shared in silence
A flicker, a spark, a guiding light

You are the painter's canvas
Where colors blend and swirl
Each stroke a testament to passion
A universe unfurled

You are the dreamer's dream
Weaving tales through endless skies
A place where wishes take their flight
Awakening with hopeful sighs